The Hagley Museum Guide

GREENVILLE · WILMINGTON · DELAWARE

ILLUSTRATION ACKNOWLEDGMENTS

Robert C. Lautman, front cover, back cover, title page, 6–7, 8, 11, 14, 17, 19 bottom, 21, 24, 25, 34, 36 bottom, 39, 41, 46, 49, 52, 55, 56, 59 top, 59 bottom left; Hagley Museum, 3, 16, 20, 42 top, 61, cover maps, floor plans; Lewis Rumford II, 13; Oliver Evans, *The Young Mill-wright & Millers Guide*, 15; Eleutherian Mills Historical Library, 18, 27, 28, 29, 30, 31, 33, 36 top, 42 bottom, 43, 44, 45, 50, 51, 57, 59 bottom right, 60, 62; C. T. Davis, *The Manufacture of Leather* (1885), 19 top; Photo Associates, 54.

FRONT COVER: The Birkenhead Roll Mills
BACK COVER: Sluice gate used to regulate the flow of water from the millrace to the waterwheel or turbine
TITLE PAGE: Overlooking the Hagley Museum Building and the Brandywine

Copyright © 1976 by the Eleutherian Mills–Hagley Foundation, Inc.
Standard Book Number 0-914650-14-9
Designed by Klaus Gemming, New Haven, Connecticut.
Composition by Finn Typographic Service, Inc., Stamford, Connecticut.
Printed by Lebanon Valley Offset Company, Inc., Annville, Pennsylvania.

TABLE OF CONTENTS

Useful Information for Visitors   *4*
Introduction   *6*
Hagley Museum Building   *9*
    First Floor Exhibits   *11*
    Second Floor Exhibits   *23*
    Third Floor Exhibits   *33*
Black Powder Exhibit Building and Walking Tour   *35*
Power in the Power Yards   *47*
Upper Property   *53*
Eleutherian Mills Historical Library   *62*
Index   *63*

Map of Museum Property: *inside front cover*
Walking Tour Map of Hagley Yard: *inside back cover*

The three basic types of waterwheels:
overshot, breast, undershot.

USEFUL INFORMATION FOR VISITORS

Hours

Open Tuesdays through Saturdays and holidays, 9:30 a.m. to 4:30 p.m., and Sundays, 1:00 p.m. to 5:00 p.m. Closed Mondays (except national holidays), Thanksgiving, Christmas, and New Year's Day. The Upper Property, including the Eleutherian Mills Residence, is open seasonally in spring and fall and during the Christmas week.

Information

Information is available at the reception desk in the Hagley Museum Building and the Museum Store. Telephone (302) 658-2401. Guides are stationed in exhibition buildings to answer questions.

Group Tours

Reservations are required for all groups. Group visits may be arranged by telephoning the Tour Office, Hagley Museum (302) 658-2401. Guides must accompany all groups touring the museum buildings and grounds. Tour duration is approximately two hours. There is a fee for group tours, which includes jitney transportation and guide. Special openings of the Residence may be arranged. Schools should request a copy of the Hagley's *Handbook for Teachers,* which describes in detail the tours available for school groups as well as other educational services.

Jitney

Buses and open-air jitneys are available to transport visitors through the property on a twenty-minute, three-mile round trip. When the Upper Property is open, it may be reached only by the use of open-air jitney or bus.

Walking Tour

Those wishing to walk through the Hagley Yard may follow the clearly marked paths of the Walking Tour described on pages 37–43 of this book. A separate brochure with map is available at the reception desk. Comfortable walking shoes are recommended. Bicycling is not allowed on the Museum grounds.

Lost and Found

Lost and found articles should be reported at the reception desk in the Hagley Museum Building.

Museum Store

A museum store is located in the small stone structure adjacent to the Hagley Museum Building. A large selection of books on American history, history of technology, decorative arts, gardens, and local wildlife, as well as gifts specifically designed for the Museum, are on sale.

Food Service

Light snacks and beverages are available from vending machines located in the Carriage Shed at the upstream end of the main parking lot. Limited picnicking facilities are provided for Museum visitors at the southwest corner of the main parking lot.

Rest Rooms

Rest rooms are located in the basement of the main Museum Building (access to the Ladies' Room is by the stairs to the left of the reception desk and to the Gentlemen's Room by the stairs at the back of the first floor), and in the Tannery Building opposite the Black Powder Exhibit Building. On the Upper Property a Ladies' Room is located on the first floor of the Residence with access by the side door, and the Gentlemen's Room is in the basement of the First Office.

INTRODUCTION

The Hagley Museum, encompassing the E. I. du Pont de Nemours & Company's original powder works, was established in 1952 on the occasion of the company's 150th anniversary. The Museum, together with the nearby Eleutherian Mills Historical Library, constitute the Eleutherian Mills-Hagley Foundation, a nonprofit, educational corporation. The original purpose of the Foundation, the preservation and interpretation of the powder mills and of Du Pont Company records, has been greatly expanded to include a much broader range of exhibits, collections, and enterprises. The Museum uses artifacts, dioramas, working models, architectural restorations, archeological remains, and publications to interpret American industrial growth during the eighteenth and nineteenth centuries.

On entering the Museum grounds, the visitor passes through the iron gates installed to commemorate the company's centennial in 1902 and drives a short distance along the Brandywine to the main Museum Building, which was

constructed in 1814 as a cotton mill. Adjacent to the Museum Building is a small stone structure, now the Museum Store, which was once a picker house where raw cotton was processed for spinning.

Eleuthère Irénée du Pont, commonly called Irénée, erected two separate powder yards upstream from the Museum Building: at Hagley and Eleutherian Mills. Hagley, perhaps named by its original owners for an estate in England, may be visited by jitney or on foot. It contains the Black Powder Exhibit Building, an operating hydroelectric exhibit, and several outdoor restorations including a waterwheel, a turbine-operated rolling mill, a dry table, and a stone quarry.

Farther upstream jitney riders will pass through an undeveloped buffer zone and enter Eleutherian Mills, where Irénée first began making black powder in 1804. Here during spring and fall openings visitors may tour the Residence and garden of Irénée du Pont, the First Office, the Barn, a cooper's shop, and a small workshop-laboratory. In addition to exhibits concerning life in this industrial community, the Museum grounds are also a wildlife preserve where hundreds of Canada geese have made their permanent home.

Hagley
Museum
Building

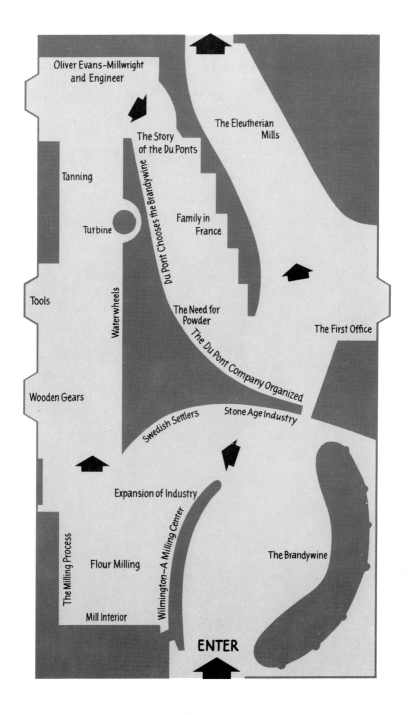

FIRST FLOOR EXHIBITS

Exhibits on the first floor of the Hagley Museum Building tell the story of the eighteenth- and early-nineteenth-century harnessing of the Brandywine, a substantial power source in the era when industry relied on waterpower. Here a series of entrepreneurs built mills to produce a variety of consumer goods from flour, cotton, and paper to linseed oil, snuff, and gunpowder.

Rising in the Welsh Mountains of Pennsylvania, the two streams that make up the Brandywine flow through rich farmland before converging near Lenape, Pennsylvania, to form a more powerful stream. As the river surges through Delaware's hills it gains momentum, its daily volume of 60,000 tons of water dropping 125 feet in the last five miles. This power of falling water was the power to do work, to

Close-up of the Brandywine Valley map
showing the powder mills and early textile mills.

produce goods, to create economic prosperity, and to inspire technological advance: the power to help build a nation.

First Settlers   The first permanent settlers to recognize the potential of the Brandywine were the Swedes, who sailed up the Delaware River in 1638 and built Fort Christina. Prior to the Swedish settlement, Lenape Indians had lived in the Brandywine Valley. They relied on their own muscle as a source of power and did not exploit the river except for fishing. In 1651 Johan Rising, the last of the Swedish governors, impressed by the promise of the Brandywine, observed that "there are water-falls; and at the most important one, called the great fall . . . could be placed . . . a flour mill, a saw-mill, and a chamois-dressing mill. . . . Besides this . . . if we could here establish powder-mills it would bring us great profit."

Swedish control of the Brandywine was short-lived, passing first to the Dutch in 1655 and then to the English in 1664. With British control came prosperity, and Rising's dreams were eventually realized. Millers such as Oliver Canby, Thomas Shipley, Joseph Tatnall, and Thomas Lea built flour mills along the Brandywine at present-day Wilmington. Founded in 1731 by Thomas Willing, Wilmington was well situated in relation to waterpower, fertile farmlands, and well-traveled trade routes. Beginning with Canby in 1742, Wilmington's mills grew in number. By 1815 Wilmington boasted fourteen mills capable of grinding 50,000 bushels of grain per year. Famous for its purity and whiteness, Brandywine flour reached domestic and foreign markets early in the century: Boston, New York, and Charleston; St. Kitts and Martinique; Lisbon, Antwerp, Londonderry, and Belfast; Calcutta and Java.

Flour Milling   Prior to the Industrial Revolution, the technique of flour milling relied heavily on manual labor. When grain arrived at the mill by wagon, it was hoisted to the loft where it was screened and cleaned. A section of the interior of an eighteenth-century gristmill originally located on Red Clay Creek at Greenbank, Delaware, shows the grinding process. Powered by water, the upper stone revolved over a stationary lower stone, pulverizing grain fed from the hopper overhead. After grinding, the meal, which had become moist

The Brandywine flour mills below Market Street,
oil painting by Bass Otis, ca. 1840.

and warm during processing, was hoisted to the floor above
where it was cooled, dried, bolted or sifted, and packaged.

In the 1790s, flour production was revolutionized by the
introduction of an early form of automation. Based on pat-
ents granted the Delaware-born engineer-millwright Oliver
Evans, mechanized milling processes reduced the amount
of heavy physical labor that characterized the "old process."
Driven by waterpower, Evans's devices provided for both
vertical and horizontal movement. Elevators, endless belts
with attached wooden or metal cups, and descenders, broad
strips of canvas or leather running over rollers and activated
by the weight of the grain, moved vertically. Horizontal
movement was achieved by belt conveyors, an endless metal
screw, or an octagonal shaft with small paddles arranged
screw-fashion along its length. Another of his improvements

An old-style gristmill required many men and much physical labor.

was the "hopper boy." This device automatically spread the milled flour on the clean floor, stirring it gently while cooling. The introduction of these processes reduced the labor force of a flour mill by one-half, and the conception of a continuous flow of material contributed to the development of mass production. Evans also experimented with steam engines, and by 1802 he had successfully harnessed steam to power a small mill for grinding plaster of Paris.

Water Power

The Brandywine was important to industrial development because it was a source of waterpower. Millwrights constructed dams to improve the fall of water, which flowed to waterwheels through millraces regulated by sluice gates. Systems of gears then transferred the power from the wheels into the various types of motion necessary to run machinery.

Diagram of a mechanized flour mill designed by Oliver Evans.

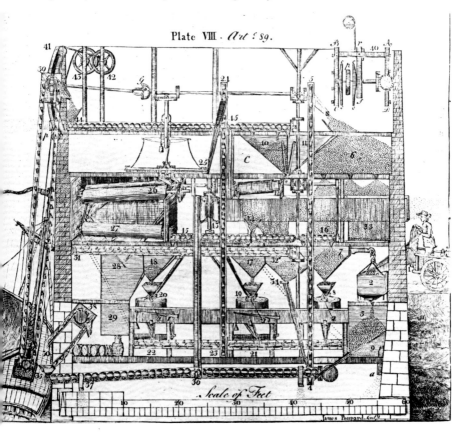

Waterwheels varied according to the height of fall from a race to the Brandywine. Breast wheels were generally used in the powder mills, but occasionally the fall was sufficient to make practicable an overshot wheel.

In the mid-nineteenth century the waterwheel gave way to the hydraulic turbine. The turbine, with its more complete and economical use of the power source, was far more efficient than the waterwheel. Consisting of a series of curved vanes rotating on a central spindle, the turbine was enclosed in a casing which channeled the water more effectively. Furthermore, the turbine could operate efficiently in high backwater when the waterwheel would be nearly stalled. The first industrially successful turbine was built in 1827 by a Frenchman, Benoit Fourneyron. The first Brandywine turbine was installed by Ellwood Morris, a Philadelphia engineer, in the nearby Rockland cotton mills in 1842, and the first turbine was put to work in the Du Pont mills in 1843.

Tanning Industry In the 1830s Wilmington's tanning industry rivaled its flour, textile, and paper production. With a good supply of water, oak bark, and grazing land for cattle, the area had

Below: *fire insurance map of R. and A. Dawes's property at Hagley in 1797.* Opposite: *millrace and sluice gates with powder mills in the background.*

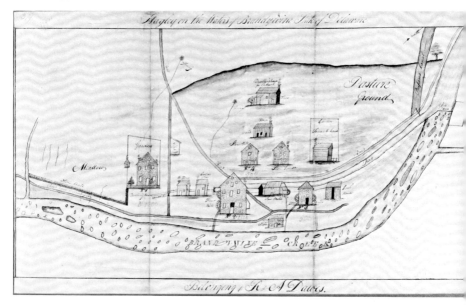

The cotton mills along the Brandywine at Rockland, Delaware, in 1870.

been an important tanning center since the mid seventeenth century. The introduction of synthetics eventually altered the industry, but Wilmington remained a leader in processing and finishing hides until the turn of the twentieth century.

Tanning relied on water for processing as well as for providing power. To facilitate scraping, skins were soaked in lime solutions to open pores and raise hairs. Following cleaning, the hides were tanned by steeping them in pits of water with bark which had been ground in water-powered bark mills.

From 1816 to 1825 a tannery and morocco-leather factory was operated in the Hagley powder yard by Alexandre Cardon de Sandrans, who was associated with relatives and business associates of Irénée du Pont. Here a new method for curing hides was employed that radically shortened the processing time from two years to two months.

Top: *workmen preparing hides for tanning in a late-nineteenth-century beam house.* Bottom: *early-nineteenth-century tan yard.*

E. I. du Pont and Gunpowder

The production of gunpowder was another important chapter in the story of the growth of American industry. One of the largest manufacturers of powder was Irénée du Pont. Du Pont, his brother Victor, and their families had come to America in 1800 with their father Pierre Samuel du Pont de Nemours, a well-known French bureaucrat and economist, on his flight from post-Revolutionary France. The family had planned to establish a rural community in America based on the father's physiocratic principles of the supremacy of land ownership and agriculture, but when it became apparent that this plan could not be realized, other means of earning a livelihood were explored. It was decided that Irénée, who had worked in the French government's black-powder manufactory under the supervision of the famous chemist Antoine Lavoisier, should open such a factory in America. Encouraged by A. Louis de Tousard, inspector of artillery to the United States Army, du Pont began a search for a suitable site.

In 1802 Irénée purchased land on the Brandywine and began construction of powder mills, a home, and a garden.

The Du Pont powder mills, crayon sketch by Pierre Gentieu, 1878.

Diorama of Eleutherian Mills about 1806.

Not only did two of the basic natural resources for powder making exist here, waterpower and willow trees for making charcoal, but the other ingredients of sulphur and saltpeter could easily be shipped up the Delaware River to Wilmington. The city was also the home of a sizable community of French émigrés.

Believing that the owner's residence should overlook the entire factory area in the French manner, Irénée built his house, now known as Eleutherian Mills, on the hillside above the new powder mills. His home was completed in 1803.

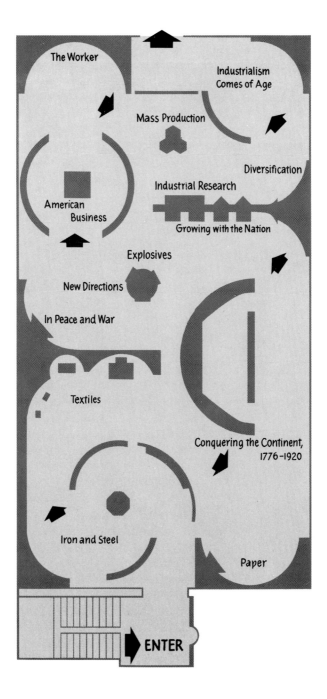

The Worker

Industrialism
Comes of Age

Mass Production

Diversification

Industrial Research

American
Business

Growing with the Nation

Explosives

New Directions

In Peace and War

Textiles

Conquering the Continent,
1776–1920

Iron and Steel

Paper

ENTER

SECOND FLOOR EXHIBITS

Exhibits on the second floor of the Museum continue the story of the industrial development of the United States. Here the scene expands beyond the Brandywine to trace the rapid growth of a new industrialism. By the end of the nineteenth century, mass-production techniques and a corporate economy characterized American manufacture. The wood technology which had supported the American colonies could not provide the machines and materials needed by the expanding nation. With mushrooming production dependent on tools, factory buildings, and railroads, the iron and steel industry became of major importance to the nation's economy.

Iron and Steel

Iron making in America dates back to 1644. By the time of the Revolution, there were ironworks in every colony except Georgia. Most of these eighteenth-century mills, like the slitting mill located at Hagley prior to Irénée's ownership, were small, and their output was often insufficient to meet local needs.

In 1810 Jesse Kersey and Isaac Pennock began the Brandywine Iron Works, the first large iron mill along this stream. Later incorporated as the Lukens Iron and Steel Company, it was among the earliest manufacturers of boilerplate in America. A replica of the rolling mill used by this firm about 1815 illustrates the making of iron plate: iron ingots were heated, rolled between heavy iron rolls, and cut to size. This mill has long since been replaced by larger, more sophisticated machinery as Lukens has grown into a giant industrial complex.

Iron and steel are made from three ingredients: iron ore, limestone, and either charcoal, coal, or coke. Small variances in the amount of carbon in iron cause significant differences in the properties of the metal. Wrought iron contains only traces of carbon and is relatively soft and malleable — suitable for forming under the hammer into horseshoes, hinges, and the like. Cast iron, high in carbon, is hard but brittle and well suited to casting into detailed

23

The Lukens mill on the Brandywine, where wrought iron was rolled into sheets.

forms. With a carbon content falling somewhere between that of wrought iron and cast iron, steel combines the toughness of one with the hardness of the other. Over the years, advances in technology from the bloomery and the blast furnace to the Bessemer and the open-hearth process have improved and increased the production of iron and steel. These developments in metallurgy in the nineteenth century revolutionized established industries and created new ones.

Textiles   The textile industry was among the first to become mechanized. It was the development of this industry that triggered the Industrial Revolution in Britain. For centuries the textile industry had been home-centered, but with the introduction of semiautomated machines for carding, spinning, and weaving, the industry began to move out of

24

Model of an early-nineteenth-century cotton mill.

the home and into the factory. Because cotton fibers are easier to process mechanically than wool, change came first to the cotton industry. Inventions such as John Hargreaves's spinning jenny (1764), Richard Arkwright's water frame (1769), and Samuel Crompton's mule (1779), revolutionized the spinning process. Weaving was similarly altered by John Kay's flying shuttle (1733) and Edmund Cartwright's power loom (1785). Beginning in England, the revolution in textile manufacturing spread to America in the years following the War for Independence.

The Brandywine was the site of numerous textile mills. The first cotton spinning mill on the stream was built by Jacob Broom in 1795 on the Eleutherian Mills site. Cotton production along the Brandywine reached its peak during the War of 1812 when twenty-seven mills with 25,000 spindles were operating within twenty miles of Wilmington. Following the war, English manufacturers dealt a heavy blow to the American textile industry by glutting the market with large quantities of underpriced goods. Although small cotton mills continued to operate along the Brandywine throughout the century, it was the large and heavily capitalized enterprises such as Lowell, located on the Merrimack River in Massachusetts, that were most successful. The present Hagley Museum Building was constructed in 1814–15 as a cotton spinning mill by Du Planty, McCall & Company. Passing under the management of several owners, the building was taken over by the Du Pont Company in 1884 and converted to the production of metal powder kegs.

Wool as well as cotton was made into cloth in Brandywine mills. Merino sheep, known for their long fleece which produced woolen cloth of high quality, were introduced into America as early as 1793 and to the Brandywine in 1805 by Irénée du Pont. Don Pedro, the ram he purchased in that year, sired many progeny and gained agricultural fame before its death in 1811. A weathervane depicting this prize Merino surmounts the cupola of the Museum Building, and his statue is displayed on the second floor. In 1810 Irénée, his brother Victor, and his

Don Pedro, Irénée du Pont's prize Merino ram.

business associates Peter Bauduy and Raphael Du Planty organized a woolen mill across the stream from the Hagley mills at Louviers. The first cloth—a quality broadcloth—was produced in 1811. It was not many years, however, before economic considerations forced a change to a cheaper, low-grade kersey cloth. The woolen mill continued under various managements into the middle of the nineteenth century. Although the Delaware industry accounted for only about 1 percent of national woolen production, the problems it faced were characteristic of those facing most American enterprises: acquiring capital, organizing business, procuring raw materials, and merchandizing in competition with British producers.

Paper Manufacturing

Paper manufacturing was another Brandywine industry to undergo partial mechanization early in the nineteenth century. In 1817 Joshua Gilpin, the earliest papermaker on the Brandywine, and his brother, Thomas, installed the first automatic paper machine to be used in America. Based on European prototypes, their machine produced continuous rolls of paper rather than individual sheets. No longer was the size of a sheet dictated by the frame in which it was formed by the laborious, time-consuming hand process. Papermaking machines increased productivity and decreased cost. They also had a considerable

Paper mold with raised watermark and removable deckle, or frame.

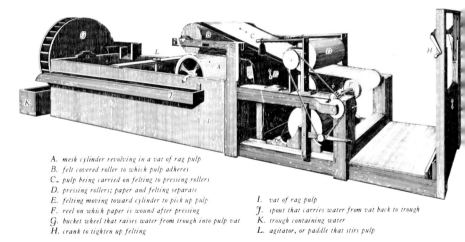

A. *mesh cylinder revolving in a vat of rag pulp*
B. *felt covered roller to which pulp adheres*
C. *pulp being carried on felting to pressing rollers*
D. *pressing rollers; paper and felting separate*
E. *felting moving toward cylinder to pick up pulp*
F. *reel on which paper is wound after pressing*
G. *bucket wheel that raises water from trough into pulp vat*
H. *crank to tighten up felting*

I. *vat of rag pulp*
J. *spout that carries water from vat back to trough*
K. *trough containing water*
L. *agitator, or paddle that stirs pulp*

*America's first paper-making machine, invented
and patented by Thomas Gilpin in 1816.*

effect on related crafts and industries. The potential of
continuous-roll paper led to innovations in such related
manufactures as wallpaper, newspaper, and books. A
change in the basic ingredient of papermaking from cotton
rag to the cheaper wood pulp around mid-century further

increased the output of paper mills, although chemicals required in the latter process produce a paper of inferior quality and stability.

Geographical Expansion

Geographical boundaries were thrust back by a fast-growing population eager to tame new territories and harvest virgin lands. As the number of Americans grew, so did the need for industry—industry to produce the materials essential to the settlement of the wilderness. Thomas Jefferson, the third president of the United States, steered the course of seventeen states. The eighth president of the United States, Martin Van Buren, presided over twenty-six states. By the eve of the Civil War this number had grown to thirty-three, and by 1900 it had swelled to forty-five. Completion of the continental borders followed in 1912.

Explosives Industry

The explosives industry grew rapidly with the expanding nation. Powder was not restricted to wartime service. As blasting powder, it was essential for such peacetime activities as clearing land for agriculture, building transportation systems, and mining natural resources. This in-

Using explosives in mining sodium nitrate, Chile, late nineteenth century.

Early Du Pont powder can.

dustry experienced changes paralleling those in textiles and iron and steel. Facilities were enlarged, production expanded, and experimentation and research undertaken.

The Du Pont Company became the largest powder manufacturer in America under the leadership of Irénée's son Henry (1850–89). During the presidencies of T. Coleman du Pont (1902–15) and Pierre S. du Pont (1915–19), great-grandsons of the founder, the company was incorporated and manufacturing expanded to include many new chemical products. Following World War I, for which the Du Pont Company supplied 40 percent of all the explosives used by the Allied forces, a conscious policy of diversification transformed the company into a leading producer of industrial chemicals and materials for the fabrication of consumer goods.

Production Technology   The energies that settled new frontiers gave impetus to a new technology whose expanded production encouraged larger and more complex organizations. The increased capital requirements of the new technology led to a re-organization of manufacturers. The gun-making and clock-making industries pioneered the techniques of the new industrialism, whose key components were interchange-able parts and an assembly-line process. Techniques of mass production were developed through the increased use of machines and the careful planning of tasks carried out by workmen. For example, in 1914 an assembly line at the Henry Ford Motor Company's Highland Park Plant had reduced the assembly time of a Model T from twelve-and-one-half man-hours to just an hour and a half. There were exceptions, but in general the single entrepreneur gave way to the partnership, and the partnership gave way to the corporation. By the 1870s the corporation was becoming the dominant form of business organization in the United States.

Despite the adoption of new and more sophisticated *Labor* power sources, manpower remained the backbone of industrial growth. As the need for workers grew, waves of immigrants swelled the ranks of the American labor force.

Powdermen, photograph by Pierre Gentieu.

They came first from northern Europe and later from southern and eastern Europe, all seeking a "better life." Approximately 31 million people immigrated to America between 1850 and 1920.

Industrialization brought both benefit and hardship to the worker. Relationships between worker and employer became increasingly impersonal, and work became more routine and monotonous as machine operators replaced craftsmen. Immigrants from all over Europe crowded into cities and mill towns. Living and working conditions deteriorated for many. To win his ultimate goal—a full share of American life—the industrial worker had to achieve a series of preliminary objectives: recognition of unions, improved working conditions, higher wages, factory legislation, shorter hours, unemployment insurance, and other benefits. Through the combined impact of organized labor, government legislation, and enlightened business leadership, the lot of the worker was gradually improved.

More and more products were made by fewer and fewer producers, because only large corporations could take advantage of mass-production methods. By the 1920s—at the end of World War I—the United States was a world leader in processing raw materials into commodities for man's use: iron and steel, paper and leather, flour and textiles. Through invention and innovation, through experimentation and diversification, American industry had expanded beyond the banks of its streams and rivers—beyond the banks of the Brandywine—to embrace world markets. Industrialism had come of age.

THIRD FLOOR EXHIBITS

Changing exhibits devoted to industrial themes are installed in the third floor exhibition area.

Two Wilmington school children enjoying the "Artisans and Architecture" exhibit.

Black Powder Exhibit Building.

Unrestored powder mills along the Brandywine.

Black Powder Exhibit Building and Walking Tour

Workmen moving powder from incorporating mills to press house by handcar.

Section of the partially restored narrow-gauge railroad.

. . . of saltpeter take seven parts, five of hazel
charcoal, and five of sulphur, and you will make
thunder and a bright light, if you know the trick.
(Trans. from Roger Bacon, ca. 1249)

Built in 1858 as a machine shop for the construction and repair of powder-yard machinery and vehicles, the Black Powder Exhibit Building is a barrel-roofed granite and timber structure whose exterior has been restored to its original appearance. In the south wing of the building scale models illustrate the process sequence of black-powder manufacture as it was practiced by Irénée du Pont. The north wing of the building serves as an auditorium for an audio-visual introduction to the history of the property and other special presentations.

Following a tour of the Black Powder Exhibit Building, visitors can walk at their leisure through the Hagley Yard and see restored powder-processing structures in operation as well as partially restored and unrestored building sites. The Walking Tour is detailed in a brochure available for a nominal charge at the reception desks in the Museum Building and the Black Powder Exhibit Building. For the visitor's convenience a Walking Tour map keyed to the discussion of the Black Powder Exhibit Building is reproduced inside the back cover. In order to understand better the powder-making process, it is suggested that the visitor tour the Black Powder Exhibit Building before the property, where the buildings occur in seemingly random fashion. This unstructured pattern resulted from innovation and changes in process, increasing production demands, and the necessity that certain buildings be located near a power source. In the mid-nineteenth century, a narrow-gauge railroad was installed to link this complex. Today a boxcar and two handcars on 400 feet of track may be seen in the Hagley Yard (9).

Eleutherian Mills, separated from the Hagley property by a buffer zone, is not open for walking but may be toured by jitney.

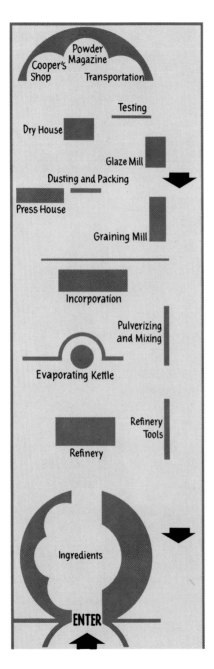

BLACK POWDER EXHIBITS

Model of Irénée du Pont's refinery where saltpeter and sulphur were purified.

Black powder was made from saltpeter, sulphur, and charcoal. Of these three ingredients, two had to be imported. Saltpeter (potassium nitrate) was dug in Bengal and shipped from Calcutta, while sulphur came from Sicily in a partially refined state. The third ingredient, charcoal, was produced locally by the controlled burning in the charcoal house of willow branches grown on or near the property. *Ingredients of Black Powder*

The first step in the production process was the refining of the saltpeter and the sulphur. This procedure was crucial, for the quality of powder depended upon the degree of refinement of the ingredients. A model of Irénée du Pont's refinery, based on early drawings and archaeological excavations, traces the purification processes. Built in 1802 and enlarged as needs dictated, the building is no longer extant. In it, crude sulphur was heated in closed iron vessels called retorts. Passing from a liquid into a gas, it recondensed as a purified liquid that solidified as it cooled. Saltpeter was also refined here. It was boiled in large kettles with water and a small amount of glue. Some *Refinery*

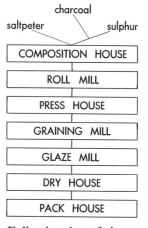

Process sequence in manufacturing black powder.

impurities floated to the top and were skimmed off, while the heavier, unwanted salts fell to the bottom as residue. The purified, liquid saltpeter was then decanted and cooled in rectangular vats. Now white and solidified, the pure saltpeter was washed, dried, and ready for pulverizing.

Composition House Following the refining process, the sulphur and the charcoal were blended in the pulverizing mill to form a mixture called "dust." The dust and the saltpeter were then stored separately in the Composition House (17). From there they were weighed and taken to the incorporating mills as needed. The danger of explosion inherent in the production of powder was responsible for the architectural peculiarities of powder mills. These buildings were constructed of three heavy stone walls with a fourth wall facing the stream and roof of a lighter material. The purpose of this design was to channel the force of an explosion across the water, safeguarding nearby powder-laden structures.

Roll Mills Because black powder is a mixture, not a compound, a thorough mixing is essential. In the earliest process used by Irénée du Pont, the ingredients were incorporated in a stamping mill, where large water-powered pestles stamped the mixture in mortars. Water was added periodically to reduce the danger of explosion. In 1822 stamping mills began to be replaced by more efficient roll mills, where huge cast-iron wheels ground the ingredients into a more homogeneous mix. There are no stamping mills in operation today on the Hagley property, although the oldest mill in the Yard, the upstream mill located at (10) on the Walking Tour, was originally built in 1814 for this purpose.

Water-powered stamping mills were first used to mix the ingredients of black powder.

Roll mills became the most numerous buildings (4, 5, 6, 13). As originally constructed, they were powered by a waterwheel placed between each pair of mills, but they were later modernized and converted to turbine power. The Eagle Roll Mills (3), named for Du Pont's Eagle Powder brand, were constructed in 1839 and rebuilt in 1886. One mill of this pair, restored to its turbine-powered state, is operated for the public at scheduled intervals throughout the day. This mill contains the Yard's only surviving roll wheels.

After incorporation, the powder "wheelcake" was taken to the press house where it was pressed hydraulically to increase its density (21). Such press cakes were then broken into chunks in the chip-roll machine and carted to the corning or graining mills (12). Here the powder chunks were reduced to grains that were sorted by size. Coarser varieties would be marketed for cannon and blasting; the finer powders went for small arms. In the next stage of processing, the powder was tumbled in glazing barrels to round the grains (11). Beginning in the 1850s, graphite was added to the barrels to make the powder shiny. The

Press House

Graining Mills

Glazing Mills

Bolters, used to sift the ingredients for making black powder.

Dry House   powder was then sent to the heated dry house to remove moisture previously introduced in the incorporation process (14). The Steam Engine House (15) contained the engine and boilers that generated steam used to heat the dry houses and to run the engine powering the machinery in the pack house. An alternate means of removing mois-

Dry Tables   ture was afforded by dry tables (20), where powder was spread in the sun to dry. When not in use, the tables were disassembled and stacked.

Pack House   In the pack house (16, 19), powder was given a final screening to remove any traces of dust created in the earlier

A Conestoga wagon in the Hagley Yard.

processing. The powder was then packaged in wrappers, metal canisters, and wooden kegs, which were made in the cooper's shop. After packaging, the powder was shipped by Conestoga wagons and by ocean-going vessels to distant ports. Following the Civil War, the railroad replaced the wagon as the major means of transport. Powder rejected because of sizing was stored in the Sweepings Room (18) to await recycling.

Sweepings Room

An exhibit demonstrating the techniques used to quarry Brandywine granite for mills and homes.

Opposite the Black Powder Exhibit Building is a stone quarry where demonstrations of drilling, cutting, and transporting stone are scheduled at regular intervals (24). The quarry was one of several on the property from which building stone was taken for industrial and domestic structures.

Stone Quarry

Other
Buildings

Within view, but not open to the general public, are several buildings of interest because of their relation to the powder-manufacturing complex: the Blacksmith Shop, the Belin House, the Gibbons/Stewart House, and the Brandywine Manufacturers' Sunday School. The stone Blacksmith Shop, built prior to 1834 as an iron shop and foundry, now houses Foundation personnel. The Belin House, the white frame residence up the hill from the Blacksmith's Shop, was constructed in 1810 with wings added later in the century. During the nineteenth century, this structure served as housing for the company's chief accountant. Opposite the Belin House is a distinctive, one-story, stone structure, the Brandywine Manufacturers' Sunday School. Built with funds and on land donated by Irénée du Pont, the school was completed in 1817. Conducted originally in a private home and then in a mill building, the Sunday School provided the only formal education available to mill workers'

Brandywine Manufacturers' Sunday School. The pollarded willow trees in the foreground were a source of wood for the charcoal used in powder making.

The Gibbons / Stewart House, a foreman's home, adjacent to the powder yards.

children. At its height, some 200 pupils regularly attended the school, held every Sunday. Du Pont's eldest daughter, Victorine, played a leading role in the school.

Children came to the school from homes such as the Gibbons/Stewart House. Built after 1840, the now isolated house is all that remains of a cluster of closely built workers' communities. Row houses sharing common walls once crowded the hillsides on both sides of the Brandywine. A magazine described one such village in 1895 as "homes piled high among the rocks, in strangest confusion, as if an avalanche of trim white houses & giant boulders had started down the hill & stopped half way, suddenly struck motionless in their mad descent."

Now used in connection with the Museum's school program, the Gibbons/Stewart House and the Brandywine Manufacturers' Sunday School provide facilities for students to participate in "living history."

Power in the
Powder Yards

In the restored area of the powder yards at their original locations the visitor may see examples of the four principal sources of power used by the mills along the Brandywine in the nineteenth century. In addition to a waterwheel and a water turbine, a steam engine and water turbine-powered electrical generator are exhibited.

Birkenhead Waterwheel   At the Birkenhead Mills, where black powder was once incorporated, a sixteen-foot wooden breast wheel has been installed. This restoration is based upon archaeology and archival records. The wheel is appropriate for the available fall of water and power requirements of the mill.

Beginning in the 1840s the waterwheels used by the Du Pont Company were gradually replaced with more efficient and durable water turbines. Ellwood Morris, a Philadelphia engineer, installed the first turbine in the powder yards in 1843. A turbine was much smaller than a waterwheel of equivalent power; more efficient in converting the energy of falling water into usable power; and operated in backwater conditions that would stall a waterwheel. By the 1880s turbines of various types had replaced all of the waterwheels in the company's Brandywine mills.

Eagle Roll Mills Water Turbine   At the Eagle Roll Mills just downstream from the Black Powder Exhibit Building a water turbine has been installed to power the only pair of roll-mill wheels still in place on the property. It is a thirty-inch turbine of the Burnham-type, which will produce about fifty h.p. at its present site. Water enters the turbine through an original thirty-six-inch cast-iron flume pipe and a reconstructed wooden tub casing, the same arrangement of pipe and casing which channeled water to the turbine originally operating this mill. This installation is demonstrated regularly by Museum guides.

Although turbines improved upon waterwheels their utility depended upon a regular supply of water. As the number of mills increased and the available water became insufficient to meet the company's power needs, especially in periods of drought, steam engines were introduced as an alternate source of power. The first steam engine was purchased for the powder mills in 1855.

By 1874 there were seven steam engines in the Du Pont mills on the Brandywine. Among these was a small box-bed engine in the Engine House, which supplied power to the pack house, a building destroyed by an explosion in 1915.

Steam Engine House

The Engine House has been restored and supplied with a horizontal slide-valve, box-bed steam engine (maker unknown) of 1870–80 vintage that has been placed where the original engine probably stood. Alongside the engine is a boiler similar in appearance to the type used in such an installation in the 1870s. Line shafting and pulleys of the type used to transmit power to the pack house some 200 feet away contrast with the shaft and bevel-gear transmission of the same period seen at the Eagle Roll Mill.

Flume pipe and water turbine at the Eagle Roll Mills.

Steam Plant

A central steam plant was constructed in 1883–84 to provide heat and power for a number of the powder-mill operations. It was located on the hillside above the Brandywine, several hundred yards upstream from the present Museum Building. This structure housed a large Corliss steam engine and three coal-fired boilers. The power was conveyed to other locations in the powder yard by means of shafting or steam pipes. The Steam Plant building has been restored, and plans are under way to install a power exhibit in it.

New Century Power House

In the late 1880s a new form of power was introduced in the powder yards. The first electric dynamo, used to provide current for lighting in the mills, was powered by the Corliss engine in the Steam Plant. This somewhat experimental arrangement was superseded in ca. 1900 when the company built the New Century Power House, located on the stream just below the Steam Plant. It employed three forty-four-inch Rechard water turbines to run several dynamos. Electricity from these dynamos was distributed throughout the yards using conventional wiring strung on poles. In most instances the current was used for electric

An 1870s horizontal slide-valve steam engine located in the Engine House.

The New Century Power House in 1903. The Steam Plant was located up the hill to the left of the smokestack.

lights, but there were a few electric motors in use where they posed no danger to the manufacture of explosives. This installation continued in use until about 1921.

Partly as a result of the fuel crisis of 1973, the Foundation began to consider ways of reducing its costs for fuel and electric power. A natural solution was to employ the waterpower of the Brandywine to drive a turbine-powered generator that would meet the needs of the Museum and Library. As a result of a detailed feasibility study, the New Century Power House was restored. Utilizing a twenty-eight-foot fall of water provided by the upper race, a modern Kaplan-type turbine has been installed, which alone provides as much power as the three original 1900 turbines. This turbine now turns a generator providing approximately 500 kilowatts, sufficient for the Foundation's needs, except in times of drought when the local power company substitutes for the Brandywine. An electric-power exhibit may be seen in this restored hydroelectric station.

Upper Property

The Du Pont Company's 150th anniversary marker.

In the buffer zone between Eleutherian Mills and Hagley is an iron truss bridge built in 1874 to link the mills and homes on both sides of the Brandywine. Inside the Eleutherian Mills property, the foundations of the large refinery and its adjoining structures were incorporated into a garden folly by the last owners. Across the service road from the refinery site is the Eleutherian Mills dam and race used by the first Du Pont mills. Adjoining this area is the site of the E. I. du Pont de Nemours & Company's 150th birthday celebration in 1952. A bronze portrait of the company's founder was mounted on an early powder mill-stone and placed there as a commemorative marker. This millstone is one of a pair purchased for the early mills. Its mate rests on the ground near the oldest mills on the Hagley property.

In the immediate area are two small dwellings of stone and timber construction, probably built by Jacob Broom, the previous owner, as mill workers' housing, and extensively rebuilt throughout the nineteenth century as a result of frequent powder-yard explosions. One of them stands on the foundations of the house traditionally believed to have been occupied by Irénée du Pont, his wife, and children for a year while awaiting the completion of their home. Although these structures are currently unrestored and not open to the general public, they are used in the Museum School Program's "Nineteenth Century Lifestyle" day.

The modern stone structure set into the hillside farther upstream is the Eleutherian Mills Historical Library.

Residence

For almost a century the Residence served as the hub of family business operations and social life. The house was deliberately situated close to the powder-making operations. While proximity afforded Irénée du Pont a degree of convenience in managing the business, it also exposed his home and family to the same ever-present dangers of explosion that faced his employees. In spite of precautions, blasts did occur, and the Residence sustained damage on numerous occasions. Various renovations to the dwelling, ranging from changes in floor plan and room designations to changes in interior finishing, were direct consequences of such accidents. As seen today, the Residence at Eleutherian Mills has a unique character bequeathed to it by time and the ministrations of several generations of the du Pont family.

Members of the family occupied the house from its completion in the summer of 1803 until a severe blast drove

First Office and Residence at Eleutherian Mills.

Mrs. Henry du Pont from the Residence in 1890. It remained empty until 1893, when it was converted first to a clubhouse for company workmen and later to a home for the head of the Du Pont Company's farm. In 1921 powder manufacturing was discontinued along the Brandywine, and the company decided to sell the land on which the first powder mills were located to members of the du Pont family. Henry Algernon du Pont, a grandson of the original owner, purchased the ancestral home for his daughter, Mrs. Louise Evelina du Pont Crowninshield, in 1923. Together they renovated the building, restoring portions to the earliest period of du Pont occupancy.

Parlor at Eleutherian Mills. A portrait of
P. S. du Pont de Nemours hangs above the fireplace.

President's room in the First Office, restored to the period ca. 1850.

In 1952 the Residence was given to the Eleutherian Mills-Hagley Foundation by Mrs. Crowninshield, who retained possession until her death in July 1958. The building was opened to the public for the first time in the spring of 1964. The first floor of the Residence remains much as she left it; the second floor is a series of period rooms—Federal, Empire, and Victorian—reflecting the tastes of the generations of du Ponts who lived there.

Irénée du Pont conducted his business from his home; *First Office* however, with the steady growth of the enterprise, office quarters in the house became cramped. Constructed in 1837 under the direction of Alfred Victor du Pont, the first office of the Du Pont Company was located at the northwest corner of the family home. Sometimes referred to as the Old Stone Office, it was a stone cube twenty-eight-feet square. In 1849 a fourteen-by-twenty-three foot addition was made. This served as Irénée's son Henry's office. Other additions, a vault room and a conference room, have been removed. This building remained the nerve center of the company until 1891 when a larger second office was constructed nearby. The First Office has been restored to the period of Henry du Pont's presidency, around 1850.

Garden   Located in front of and slightly to the southwest of the Residence is the garden. As soon as Irénée du Pont had acquired land on the Brandywine, he set about planting a garden and orchard to complement his home. French in character, the early garden was composed of four quadrants, each bordered by dwarf fruit trees. A drive flanked the northern perimeter. To the south and west of the garden were extensive orchards. Archaeological work has provided the basis for the current restoration of the garden as it existed during Irénée's lifetime. A gazebo built in 1817 has been reconstructed in the southwest corner of the garden. Described by Irénée's father as "a small latticed room covered by honeysuckle," it provides today, as it did then, a pleasant spot from which to contemplate the garden.

Barn   The du Pont family engaged in farming as a necessary supplement to powder-making operations. They grew willows for charcoal production; pastured the horses, mules, and oxen used in pulling the powder wagons; and raised the fodder crops for winter feeding. Irénée gave special attention to sheep raising from the time of his arrival in Delaware until about 1820, intending to furnish fine Merino fleece to his brother's woolen mill located across the Brandywine. Fuller's teasels, thistles used to raise the nap of finished woolen cloth, were also grown at Eleutherian Mills. As farming and factory operations expanded, adjacent lands were purchased or leased, and corn, oats, rye, and millet were added to the number of crops grown. These agricultural operations reached their peak in terms of land under cultivation and livestock owned during the mid nineteenth century.

The stone Barn around which the farming activities revolved was constructed at the same time that the Residence and the first mills were being built, 1802–03. Like most structures in this working complex, it too grew with time. In 1844 it was reconstructed and enlarged to its present size and appearance. The stone buttresses and other strengthening features common to the powder mills were

Exterior of the barn, enlarged to its present size in 1844.

built into the Barn to help it resist the shattering force of explosions. Today the Barn houses a selection of nineteenth-century domestic, farm, and powder-yard vehicles as well as collections of weather vanes and agricultural tools and implements.

On the lower level of the Barn, a coopering exhibit shows the crafting of wooden stave containers. The com-

Cooper Shop

Left: *a Conestoga wagon used by the Du Pont Company.*
Right: *a cooper and his powder barrels.*

Workshop of Lammot du Pont, originally located on the adjacent Nemours property.

pany maintained a cooper shop on the property throughout much of the nineteenth century to supply its continuous demand for the barrels and kegs needed to package their product.

Lammot du Pont Workshop

On the downstream side of the Residence and set back into the woods is a small frame building in the Greek Revival style. Known traditionally as Lammot du Pont's laboratory, it was moved to this site in 1968 from the neighboring property of Nemours. Within the walls of this building, the workshop of Irénée's grandson Lammot (1831–1884) has been recreated.

Lammot joined the Du Pont Company in 1850 upon graduation from the University of Pennsylvania, where he had majored in chemistry. Henry du Pont, head of the company, relied on his nephew, referring to him as "our chemist." Since the appearance of his workshop is not known, the present restoration was based upon knowledge of his technical achievements and of other nineteenth-century laboratories and workshops. The interior illustrates three aspects of Lammot's talents: inventor and engineer, architect and builder, and chemist.

Delivery wagon.

The Hagley Museum has not attempted to restore the manufacturing community that once flourished along the banks of the Brandywine. Rather, it seeks to recreate an atmosphere where the history of American industry in the nineteenth century can be understood and appreciated.

The Library building

ELEUTHERIAN MILLS
HISTORICAL LIBRARY

As a center for research, the Library concentrates on American economic, industrial, business, and technological history. Its geographical focus is Delaware, eastern Pennsylvania, southern New Jersey, and northern Maryland. An extensive collection of printed material provides an essential national context for understanding regional economic growth.

The Library's 125,000 volumes, six to seven million manuscript items, and a quarter of a million pictorial images afford a detailed historical view of nineteenth-century iron and steel, chemical, oil, tanning, shipbuilding, banking, mercantile, explosive, textile, and other industries. The archives of the Du Pont Company, 1802–1915, have been augmented by extensive du Pont family papers, beginning with Pierre Samuel du Pont de Nemours, the French physiocrat.

Although primarily organized to be of greatest assistance to advanced scholarly research, the Library welcomes any individual whose inquiry may benefit from the use of the collections.

INDEX

Barn, 7, 58–60
Bauduy, Peter, 27
Belin House, 44
Birkenhead Mills, 7, 48
Black Powder Exhibit Building, 7, 37
Black powder, 20; ingredients, 21, 39; production process, 39–43
Blacksmith Shop, 44
Brandywine flour mills, 12
Brandywine Iron Works. *see* Lukens Iron and Steel Company
Brandywine Manufacturers' Sunday School, 44–45
Brandywine River, 6, 11–12, 15, 16, 20, 26, 27, 48–49, 54, 56
Broom, Jacob, 26, 55

Canby, Oliver, 12
Cardon de Sandrans, Alexandre, 18
Carriage Shed, 5
Centennial Gates, 6
Commemorative marker, 54
Composition House, 40
Conestoga wagon, 43
Cooper's shop, 7, 59–60
Crowninshield, Louise Evelina du Pont, 56–57

Delaware River, 12
Don Pedro, 26
Dry house, 42
Dry Tables, 7, 42
Du Planty, Raphael, 27
Du Planty, McCall & Company, 26
Du Pont, Alfred Victor, 57
Du Pont, Eleuthère Irénée, 7, 18, 20–21, 26, 37, 39, 40, 44, 54, 55, 57, 58
Du Pont, Henry, 30, 57–58, 60–61
Du Pont, Henry Algernon, 56
Du Pont, Lammot, 60–61
Du Pont, Mrs. Henry, 56
Du Pont, Pierre S., 30
Du Pont, T. Coleman, 30

Du Pont, Victor, 20, 26
Du Pont, Victorine, 45
Du Pont Company, 6, 16, 20–21, 30, 48, 49, 54, 56, 57, 62
Du Pont de Nemours, Pierre Samuel, 20, 58, 62

Eagle Roll Mills, 7, 41, 48, 49
Eleutherian Mills, 7, 26, 37, 54–61; Residence, 5, 7, 21, 55–57
Eleutherian Mills–Hagley Foundation, 6, 57
Eleutherian Mills Historical Library, 6, 55, 62
Engine House, 42, 49
Evans, Oliver, 13
Explosives industry, 29–30

Farming, at Eleutherian Mills, 58
First Office (Old Stone), 5, 7, 57–58
Flour milling, 12–13
Food service, 5
Fort Christina, 12
Fourneyron, Benoit, 16

Garden, 7, 58
Gazebo, 58
Gibbons / Stewart House, 44, 45
Gilpin, Joshua and Thomas, 27
Glazing mills, 41
Graining mills, 41
Gristmill, interior, 12
Group tours, 4
Gunpowder. *see* black powder

Hagley Museum, 6
Hagley Museum Building, 5, 6–7, 26, 37, 50; exhibits in, 11–33
Hagley, powder yard, 7, 37, 54
Hours, Museum, 4
Housing, workers. *see* Gibbons / Stewart House
Hydroelectric plant. *see* New Century Power House

Incorporating mills. *see* roll mills and stamping mills
Information, 4
Iron and steel industry, 23–24

Jefferson, Thomas, 29
Jitney, 4

Kersey, Jesse, 23

Labor, 31–32
Lammot du Pont Workshop, 7, 60–61
Lavoisier, Antoine, 20
Lea, Thomas, 12
Lenape Indians, 12
Lenape, Pennsylvania, 11
Lost and found, 5
Louviers, 27
Lukens Iron and Steel Company, 23

Merino sheep, 26, 58
Morris, Ellwood, 16, 48
Museum Store, 5, 7

Narrow-gauge railroad, 37
New Century Power House, 7, 50–51

Pack house, 42–43
Papermaking, 27–29
Pennock, Isaac, 23
Powder manufacturing, along the Brandywine, 20–21
Power transmission, 49, 50–51
Press house, 41
Production technology, 30–31
Pulverizing mill, 40

Refinery: model, 39–40; ruins, 54
Rest Rooms, 5
Rising, Johan, 12
Rockland, cotton mills, 16
Rolling mill. *see* Lukens Iron and Steel Company
Roll mills, 40–41. *see also* Eagle Roll Mills
Roll wheels, 40, 41, 48

Shipley, Thomas, 12
Slitting mill, 23
Stamping mills, 40
Steam engine, 7, 15, 48–49, 50
Steam Plant, 50
Stone Quarry, 7, 43
Swedish settlers, 12
Sweepings Room, 43

Tannery Building, 18
Tanning industry, 16, 18
Tatnall, Joseph, 12
Textile industry, 24, 26
Textile mills, along the Brandywine, 26–27
Tousard, A. Louis de, 20

Van Buren, Martin, 29

Walking tour, 5, 37
Waterpower, 11, 15, 48
Water turbine, 16, 48, 50–51
Waterwheels, 16, 48. *see also* Birkenhead Mills
Welsh Mountains, 11
Willing, Thomas, 12
Wilmington, 12
Workshop. *see* Lammot du Pont Workshop